W9-AAK-777

HANDY HEALTH GUIDE TO ASTHMA

GUIDES ★ HANDY ★ HEALTH ★

Alvin and Virginia Silverstein
and Laura Silverstein Nunn

Enslow Publishers, Inc.
40 Industrial Road
Box 398
Berkeley Heights, NJ 07922
USA

http://www.enslow.com

Original edition published as *Asthma* in 2002.

Library of Congress Cataloging-in-Publication Data
Silverstein, Alvin.
Handy health guide to asthma / by Alvin Silverstein, Virginia Silverstein, and Laura Silverstein Nunn.
    p. cm. — (Handy health guides)
  Summary: "An overview of asthma for children in grades 5 and up. Find out what asthma is, what causes it, how it is
diagnosed, and some treatment options"— Provided by publisher.
Includes index.
  ISBN 978-0-7660-4269-8
1. Asthma—Juvenile literature. I. Silverstein, Virginia B. II. Nunn, Laura Silverstein. III. Title.
  RC591.S554 2013
  616.2'38—dc23

                    2012028926

Future editions:
Paperback ISBN: 978-1-4644-0481-8
EPUB ISBN: 978-1-4645-1249-0
Single-User PDF ISBN: 978-1-4646-1249-7
Multi-User PDF ISBN: 978-0-7660-5881-1

Printed in the United States of America

052013 Lake Book Manufacturing, Inc., Melrose Park, IL

10 9 8 7 6 5 4 3 2 1

To Our Readers: We have done our best to make sure all Internet Addresses in this book were active and appropriate
when we went to press. However, the author and the publisher have no control over and assume no liability for the
material available on those Internet sites or on other Web sites they may link to. Any comments or suggestions can be
sent by e-mail to comments@enslow.com or to the address on the back cover.

♻ Enslow Publishers, Inc., is committed to printing our books on recycled paper. The paper in every book contains
10% to 30% post-consumer waste (PCW). The cover board on the outside of each book contains 100% PCW. Our
goal is to do our part to help young people and the environment too!

Illustration Credits: CDC/James Gathany, p. 43; Dynamic Graphics/Photos.com, p. 41; Eye of Science/Photo
Researchers, Inc., pp. 10 (bottom), 24; © iStockphoto.com/bobbieo, p. 15; @ iStockphoto.com/FernandoAH, p. 25;
John Takai/Photos.com, p. 39; Joyce Photographics/Photo Researchers, Inc., p. 40; Kakigori Studio/Photos.com,
p. 8; Louis-Paul St-Onge/Photos.com, p. 35; Peter Gardiner/Photo Researchers, Inc., p. 36; © Science Photo Library/
Alamy, p. 33; Shutterstock.com, pp. 1, 3, 4, 6, 9, 10 (top), 11, 13, 14, 19, 21, 22, 23, 29, 30, 32, 42; Simon Fraser/Photo
Researchers, Inc., p. 26; Thinkstock Images/Photos.com, p. 18; Tim Vernon/Photo Researchers, Inc., p. 20.

Cover Photo: Shutterstock.com

CONTENTS

1 Take a Breath 5

2 How Breathing Works 7

3 What Is Asthma? 12

4 What Causes Asthma? 17

5 How Do You Know It's Asthma? 29

6 Treating Asthma 34

7 Preventing Asthma Attacks 40

Glossary 44

Learn More 47

Index 48

Sometimes it can be difficult to catch your breath.

1

TAKE A BREATH

Take a deep breath and let it out. Usually you don't have to think about breathing. In fact, you may not even realize you are doing it. Breathing becomes noticeable when you are running to catch a bus or sick with a cold.

Some people, however, have to think about breathing every single day. Sometimes they have to struggle just to take a breath. These people may have asthma.

Asthma is a condition that causes part of a person's airways (breathing passages) to become narrow, making it hard for air to get through. As a result, the person may have trouble breathing and may cough or wheeze. Tiny bits of dust, mold, or pollen in the air may bring on breathing problems. Air pollution, very cold weather, exercise, or a bad cold can also make it hard to breathe.

Asthma attacks can be very dangerous—even deadly. There is no cure, but there are ways to keep asthma under control. Symptoms can be treated with fast-acting medications. There are also some things that you can do that may prevent asthma attacks from occurring. Before you can understand what happens during an asthma attack, first you need to know how normal breathing works.

Handy Healthy Fact

Asthma on the Rise

Asthma is a common condition, affecting about 20 million Americans. Nearly 9 million of them are children. Children have smaller airways than adults, so asthma can become more serious for them. Health experts say that the number of asthma cases has increased greatly in recent years and is still on the rise.

2

HOW BREATHING WORKS

When you breathe in, or inhale, air comes in through your nose and mouth. The air then passes down into two spongy organs in your chest called lungs, which fill up with air like balloons. Inside the lungs, oxygen—an invisible gas that is part of the air—passes into your blood, which carries it to the many cells of the body. Your body needs oxygen to produce the energy you need to do things like running, playing, eating, thinking, and even sleeping. When the cells use oxygen to produce energy, they also make a gas called carbon dioxide. The blood carries carbon dioxide to the lungs, and it is pushed out when you breathe out, or exhale. When you breathe in again, the process is repeated and it brings fresh air into the lungs.

Take a Breath

The average person takes 12 to 16 breaths every minute. That's more than 20,000 breaths each day! You take even more breaths when you exercise or get stressed. But when you sleep, your breathing slows down.

The parts of the body involved in breathing make up the respiratory system. The respiratory system looks a lot like an upside-down tree. The "trunk" of the tree—the main breathing tube—is called the trachea. You can feel the trachea at the front of your throat. The air you breathe goes down your throat into your chest. There the trachea branches into two large tubes called the bronchi. These tubes lead into the lungs. The bronchi each divide into smaller, almost threadlike tubes, called bronchioles, which look like the branches of a tree.

The bronchi and bronchioles are wrapped in bands of muscle. When these muscles relax, the airways

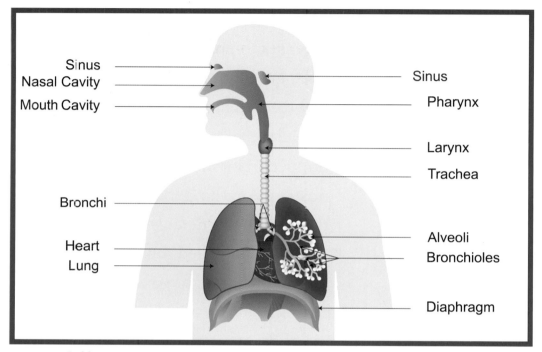

Sinus
Nasal Cavity
Mouth Cavity

Sinus
Pharynx
Larynx
Trachea

Bronchi
Heart
Lung

Alveoli
Bronchioles

Diaphragm

Many different body parts work together to help your respiratory system function properly.

widen. When they contract, or tighten, the airways narrow, and less air can flow through. Normally when you breathe, these muscles are loose and relaxed.

The bronchioles lead into millions of tiny balloon-like air sacs in the lungs. These sacs are called alveoli. They look like tiny bunches of grapes, but they are far too small to see without a microscope. This is where the exchange of oxygen and carbon dioxide takes place.

Alveoli look very much like a bunch of grapes.

The airways have built-in defenses to protect the lungs from dust and other particles that may be breathed in from the air. Some particles that enter your nose get trapped in bristly hairs inside your nostrils. Anything that gets past the first line of defense falls into a gooey liquid called mucus that covers the lining of your nose.

Mucus is also produced in the airways, and it picks up pollen grains or tiny bits of dust that might have gotten

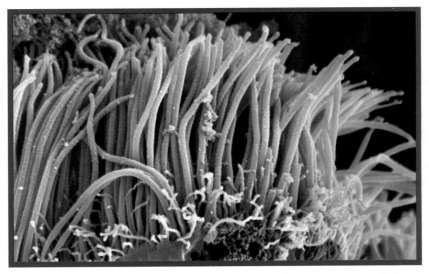

Hairlike cilia line your airways and move particles away from your lungs.

through. Some of the cells lining the airways have tiny hairlike structures called cilia that move back and forth, creating waves in the mucus coating. Like a conveyor belt, the moving mucus sweeps trapped particles up and away from your lungs. The particles leave your body when you blow your nose, sneeze, or cough. The term *asthma* is a Greek word meaning "panting."

Wind Power

You may think you're blowing hard when you're blowing out the candles on a birthday cake, but the gust of air from a cough or sneeze is even harder. When you sneeze, the air can explode out of your airways at an average speed of 40 miles (64 kilometers) per hour. But some sneezes travel even faster. A record-breaking sneeze was clocked at over 100 miles (160 kilometers) per hour! That's as powerful as the winds in a hurricane!

Handy Healthy Fact

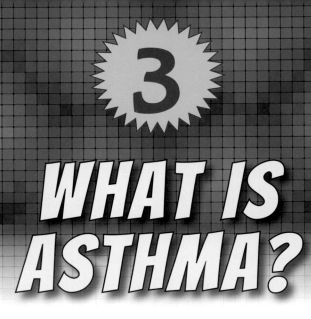

3
WHAT IS ASTHMA?

It was first used thousands of years ago to describe the wheezing sound that people make when they are having trouble breathing.

People with asthma have very sensitive airways that tend to overreact when foreign substances are breathed in. Doctors sometimes call these airways "twitchy."

What happens during an asthma attack? When the bronchial tubes are exposed to things like smoke or dust, they become irritated. This causes the muscles that wrap around the airways to tighten and prevent the particles from getting farther into the lungs. The contracting muscles make the airways narrower, leaving less room for air to get through. This effect is called a bronchospasm.

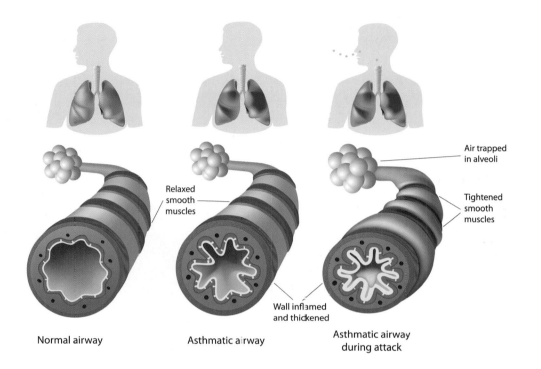

Air trapped
in alveoli

Relaxed
smooth
muscles

Tightened
smooth
muscles

Wall inflamed
and thickened

Normal airway

Asthmatic airway

Asthmatic airway
during attack

At the same time, the walls of the bronchial tubes become inflamed and swollen, making it even harder for air to flow. The inflammation causes the airways to produce a lot of extra mucus. Sometimes the mucus forms plugs in the airways, which blocks them even more.

When the airways are narrowed, breathing becomes difficult, and a person may be short of breath. Wheezing is the most obvious symptom of asthma. When air tries to squeeze through the narrow passageway, it makes a

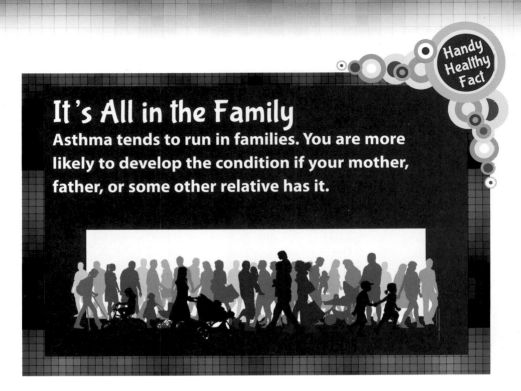

Handy Healthy Fact

It's All in the Family

Asthma tends to run in families. You are more likely to develop the condition if your mother, father, or some other relative has it.

whistling sound. But not all people with asthma wheeze, which may make it hard to identify the condition. Some people feel their chest getting tight because their lungs have to work harder than usual to push air through the narrow airways.

Coughing is the most common symptom of asthma. It may be caused by the extra mucus produced in the airways. Bronchospasm alone can also cause coughing. Unfortunately, people

Coughing is very common in people with asthma.

14

usually don't see coughing as a sign of something serious such as asthma. They may think it is caused by a cold or something that is in their throat.

Asthma symptoms vary greatly from person to person. Whether the symptoms are mild or severe depends on how seriously the airways are inflamed.

It is important to treat asthma attacks early. This helps prevent further inflammation that can make the symptoms worse. If asthma is not treated right away, the attacks may destroy some of the cilia that sweep particles away from the lungs. Then, with fewer cilia, the airway lining cannot clear out the particles as effectively.

Handy Healthy Fact

Trapped Air

People with asthma do not have a problem with breathing in, but rather breathing out. When the air comes in, it gets trapped, and a person with asthma has to struggle to push the air back out of the narrow airways.

Activity 1: Asthma Is Like Breathing Through a Straw

Did you ever try breathing through a straw? Many asthma patients say that is what it feels like when they are having an asthma attack. You can do a little experiment to get an idea of what it's like to have asthma. All you need is a straw and a watch or clock with a second hand.

• Run in place for two minutes, timing yourself with a watch or clock. When the time is up, pinch your nose and put a straw into your mouth. Then try to breathe in and out only through the straw. Now, narrow the straw by pinching it in the middle. Is it even more difficult to breathe? This is what it feels like when a person with asthma tries to breathe during an asthma attack.

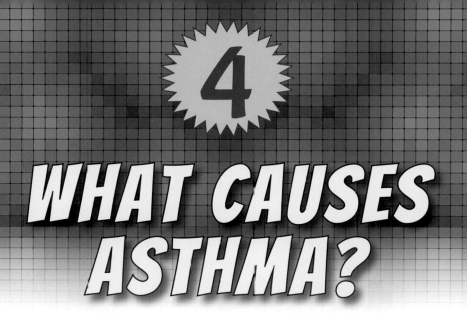

4

WHAT CAUSES ASTHMA?

No one is sure exactly what causes asthma. Scientists do know that certain things in the environment can bring on the symptoms of an asthma attack. These things are called triggers. An asthma attack usually occurs either right away or within about fifteen to thirty minutes after exposure to a trigger.

Asthma is very often linked with allergies. An allergy is an unusual reaction to a substance that is normally harmless. Most people can breathe in the summer air or play with a puppy without sneezing. But for people with allergies, these kinds of things may trigger an asthma attack.

Most people can play with animals without coughing or sneezing because they are not allergic to them.

Do germs cause allergies? Not exactly. Allergies are actually the result of a mistake by the body's own defenses. These defenses are called the immune system. Normally the immune system attacks germs that have gotten into your body. But sometimes the body's defenses confuse harmless things, like dust or tiny pollen grains from plants, with germs that could make you sick. So they go after them, the way they would attack invading germs.

White blood cells are an important part of your immune system. They are jellylike blobs that can swim easily through blood and squeeze between body cells. Some white blood cells go after germs and attack them. Others make special proteins called antibodies, which may damage the germs or make them easier to kill.

After the battle is over, some of the antibodies stay in the body. If the same kind of germs invade again, the

An Asthma–Allergy Link

About 90 percent of kids with asthma have allergy triggers. But people with allergies do not necessarily develop asthma.

cells that make antibodies will quickly make a whole new supply so they can fight the germs. As a result, the person will not get sick from the same kind of germs again. The person is now immune to that illness.

In people with allergies, the immune system makes antibodies against chemicals that would not have caused any harm. These may be chemicals on the surface of dust or pollen grains (tiny particles that flowers use to make seeds) or chemicals in foods. A substance that causes an allergic reaction is called an allergen.

You may not get a reaction the first time you are exposed to an allergen. If you eat a strawberry, for instance, your body may mistake strawberry chemicals

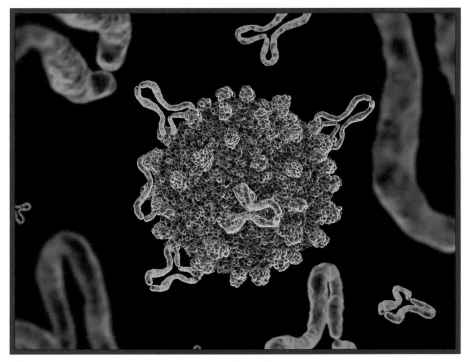

This illustration shows antibodies (green) attacking a virus.

for invaders and produce antibodies, but there won't be enough of them to bother you. The next time you eat strawberries, your body produces more antibodies. The more strawberries you eat, the worse your allergy symptoms will become. This kind of exposure buildup is called sensitization. Your body has now become sensitive to strawberries, and you will have an allergic reaction, such as an itchy rash or a stomachache every time you eat them.

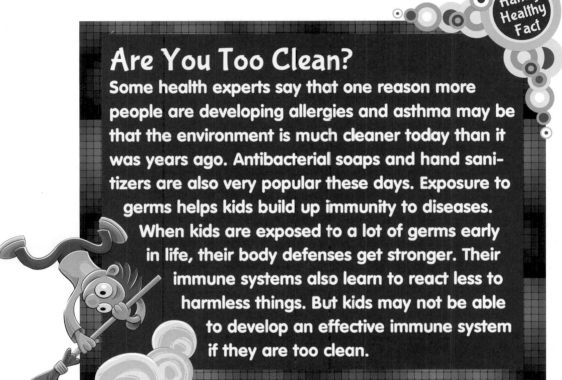

Are You Too Clean?

Some health experts say that one reason more people are developing allergies and asthma may be that the environment is much cleaner today than it was years ago. Antibacterial soaps and hand sanitizers are also very popular these days. Exposure to germs helps kids build up immunity to diseases. When kids are exposed to a lot of germs early in life, their body defenses get stronger. Their immune systems also learn to react less to harmless things. But kids may not be able to develop an effective immune system if they are too clean.

During an allergic reaction, sensitive cells in various parts of the body (such as the skin or the breathing passages) react to the combination of allergens and allergy antibodies. These body cells send out a chemical called histamine. Histamine makes cells get swollen and watery so that white blood cells can move through them more easily. Unfortunately, histamine can also cause annoying symptoms, such as a runny nose, watery

Pollen grains from flowers can cause an allergic reaction.

eyes, itching, and sneezing. Pollen is a very common trigger for people with asthma. Many people have seasonal asthma and have attacks during the "hay fever season."

Other allergens include house dust and molds, which can be found all over your house. They can be under mattresses, in closets, in carpets, or in stuffed animals.

A person who develops asthma symptoms after petting a cat or dog may be allergic to animal dander, tiny flakes of dead skin. Animals shed dander on carpets and furniture. Different animals have different dander, so you may be allergic to dogs but not to cats.

The feathers of birds also contain allergens. Mice, hamsters, and guinea pigs can be a problem as well, but the allergen from these animals is mainly in their urine. Many people are allergic to the chemicals in cockroach droppings. In cities, wild mice, rats, and cockroaches are a big cause of asthma.

Foods can bring on an asthma attack. Common food allergens include milk products, fish, peanuts and other nuts, wheat, and eggs.

Other asthma triggers may not be related to an allergy. For instance, a person with asthma may be sensitive to irritating substances—things that can

Dog hair and dander can collect on furniture and carpets.

What's in House Dust?

If you put a tiny bit of dust under a microscope, you might be surprised at what you see. House dust may include fibers from bedsheets, flakes of dead skin, pollen grains, pet hair, mold spores, and little bits of insects. Things like these could be enough to make you sneeze, but an allergy to dust may actually be caused by dust mites. These are tiny bugs that feed on dead skin flakes and other things in dust. It's usually the dust mites' droppings that cause allergy problems. They are so tiny and light that they can easily float through the air, enter your nose, and cause symptoms.

Some places in the world are asthma-free. For instance, asthma is very rare among the Eskimos in North America. That might be because the climate is too cold for dust mites to live.

Exercise is a common asthma trigger.

bother anybody, not just someone with allergies. These include air pollution, cigarette smoke, and certain chemicals in products.

A respiratory illness, such as a cold or flu, can also trigger an asthma attack. Cold weather, stress, and even crying or laughing can set off an attack.

Exercise is a common trigger for people with asthma. When people exercise, their muscles use up extra oxygen. Their lungs work harder. They breathe faster and take in more air. During exercise, the nose does not have enough time to warm up the air before it goes to the lungs. The air may be cold and dry when it gets to the lungs. The cold air entering the airways may make them suddenly get narrow.

As dry air passes through them, the airways lose the moist mucus that normally protects them. Because people with asthma have very sensitive airways, cold, dry air is more likely to bring on an attack.

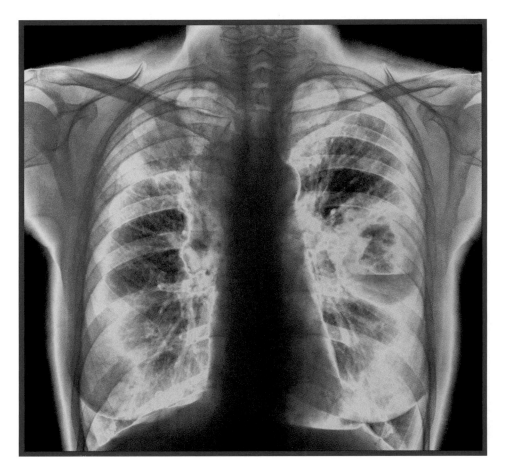

This smoker's lung is damaged from years of smoking.

The Dangers of Smoking

Everyone knows that smoking cigarettes is bad for you. When you breathe in cigarette smoke, the harmful chemicals in it—such as carbon monoxide—go right into your lungs. Carbon monoxide is very dangerous because it keeps the blood from bringing oxygen to the brain, heart, lungs, and other important organs in the body. Cigarette smoke also damages the cilia in the lining of the airways. Eventually, they are unable to sweep mucus and foreign particles out of the lungs and up toward the throat. Some chemicals in cigarette smoke stay in the lungs. They can cause some serious illnesses, such as bronchitis, emphysema, or lung cancer. If these things can happen to a person with healthy lungs, can you imagine what smoking can do to someone with asthma?

Activity 2: How Do the Airways Dry Out?

• Run the tip of your tongue over the roof of your mouth and note how moist and slippery it feels. Then breathe in and out through your open mouth (holding your nose closed) for thirty seconds. What does the inside of your mouth feel like now?

When you exercise, a lot of air flows in and out through the airways. So their moist lining dries out quickly. Here's an experiment to show you how this happens.

• Wet two sponges and squeeze them out just enough so that they are not dripping. Place one wet sponge in front of a blowing fan but keep the other one away from the flow of air. Observe each sponge every five minutes. (Look at them, feel them, and press a piece of paper towel gently against the surface of each one to see if it picks up a spot of moisture.) Note how long it takes for the surface of each sponge to get dry. You will find that the one you placed in front of the fan will dry out more quickly than the one outside the air current.

5

HOW DO YOU KNOW IT'S ASTHMA?

Asthma can be pretty tricky to detect. Many of its symptoms—coughing, wheezing, shortness of breath, chest tightness, and breathing problems—may be confused with signs of other respiratory conditions.

Asthma symptoms are also different in different people, and they may be mild or very serious. All these things may make it hard to identify the condition. Yet it is important to diagnose asthma as soon as possible so effective treatment can begin right away.

Symptoms of asthma, such as coughing and wheezing, may often be confused with other illnesses.

Keep an Asthma Diary

You can help the doctor make a diagnosis by keeping a diary of your condition. Write down as much as you can about the problem. Make sure you enter the dates and times when problems occur along with a complete description. What are the symptoms? What were you doing before they started?

An asthma diary will help the doctor and patient under-stand the illness better. That way the doctor can treat the condition more effectively.

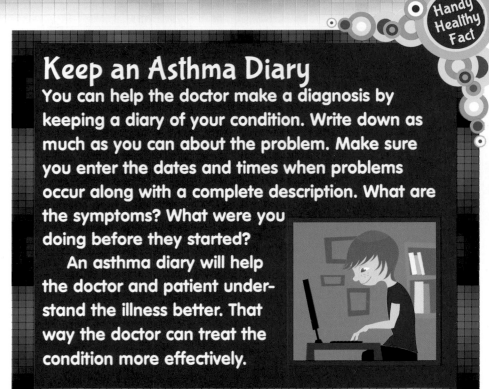

For a proper diagnosis, the first thing you need to do is go to the doctor. The doctor will ask questions about the illness and your family's medical history. Does anyone in your family have asthma or allergies? When did the breathing problems begin? What are the symptoms? How severe are they? When and where do they occur? How often do they occur? How long do they last? Does the problem get worse after exercising? Are you exposed to cigarette smoke, air pollution, or other irritants?

Asthma at Night

Some kids develop asthma symptoms at night and then feel fine during the day. This can make it hard for a doctor to diagnose the condition.

The doctor will then give you a physical exam, starting by checking your nose for signs of allergy or upper respiratory infection. He or she will check your breathing with a stethoscope. This instrument is used to listen to your heart and lungs. It helps the doctor hear if they are working properly. But if you are not having any symptoms at that moment, your breathing will probably sound normal. Sometimes, if you are having serious breathing problems, the doctor may use a chest X-ray to see if the airways are blocked. However, this test works best when it is taken while the patient is having breathing problems.

An asthma specialist may give you breathing tests using a spirometer. This instrument measures how much air flows in and out of the airways when you blow into a special tube. Then you will be given medication that opens up the airways. If the spirometer shows that the airflow is much better, this is more evidence that you have asthma.

Because allergens are one of the most common triggers of asthma, allergy testing is an important tool for diagnosis. Skin testing is used to identify the allergens that may be causing your asthma attacks. Allergens are placed on the skin, which is then scratched or pricked with a needle. Sometimes small amounts of an allergen solution are injected into the skin. If the skin becomes red or swollen within fifteen minutes, you are sensitive to that allergen.

Special blood tests can also be used to test for allergies. The RAST test measures the amounts of antibodies that are triggered by specific allergens.

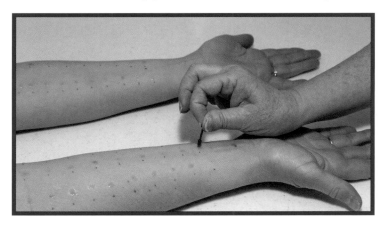

Allergens are placed on scratches on the skin to test for allergic reactions.

For instance, if you have a special antibody for dust in your blood, then you are probably allergic to dust.

There is one testing device that patients can use in their own homes—the peak flow meter. This device measures how fast air flows out of the lungs when a person exhales quickly. If the reading shows a drop in airflow, this could be a sign that an asthma attack is developing. The peak flow meter can actually show the early signs of an asthma attack even before the person is noticing breathing problems. This can help asthma patients treat the symptoms early, before they have a chance to get worse. The peak flow meter can also help diagnose kids whose asthma occurs mostly at night.

This boy is measuring how fast the air flows out of his lungs with a peak flow meter.

6
TREATING ASTHMA

There is no cure for asthma, but it can be controlled. Asthma patients need to work closely with their doctors to find a treatment plan that works best for them. Each person with asthma has different needs, so every treatment plan is different. With an effective treatment plan, people with asthma can live normal lives.

Asthma medications come in many forms, including pills, liquids, and injections. But inhalers are actually the most popular device people use for asthma treatment. That's because they are fast, easy, and handy. For severe attacks, people often use a handheld device called a nebulizer. A nebulizer sprays a mist of medication into the person's bronchial tubes. The drug works right there to open up the airways and relieve the symptoms.

Inhalers are easy to use and can be carried just about anywhere.

There are two main types of asthma medications: bronchodilators and anti-inflammatory drugs.

Bronchodilators are drugs that work by relaxing the muscles in the airways, allowing the narrowed airways to open up. Air can then flow in and out more easily, making it easier to breathe. Bronchodilators are often used to relieve symptoms just as they occur. But if the person's asthma is severe, he or she may need to take the bronchodilator regularly, even before symptoms develop. This can prevent attacks before they happen.

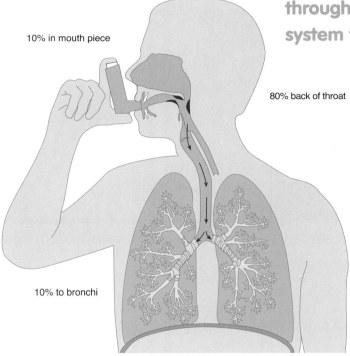

This diagram shows how bronchodilators move through the respiratory system to open airways.

10% in mouth piece

80% back of throat

10% to bronchi

Many doctors believe that it is most important to treat the main problem of asthma—inflammation of the airways. Anti-inflammatory drugs can do the job by reducing the swelling and twitchiness in the airways. These drugs are usually taken regularly, once or twice a day. Regular use of these drugs can help make the airways less sensitive and less likely to start a reaction.

Aren't Steroids Bad?

You may have heard about sports stars who take drugs called steroids to pump up their muscles. These drugs are dangerous and illegal. You may be surprised to learn, however, that some steroid drugs are used to treat asthma. These are not the same as the illegal steroids; they are anti-inflammatory drugs. When they are taken in the right amounts, under a doctor's supervision, they are safe and effective.

How do you know what type of asthma medication you need and how much? Well, that depends on how severe your symptoms are and how often they occur. People with mild asthma may need fast-acting drugs that treat the symptoms on the spot. This is good for people who don't get asthma attacks very often.

People with a more serious case may need a long-term treatment plan. They may take asthma medication every day to control inflammation and symptoms. Eventually, the person will have fewer attacks. The person should continue to take medication, however, to keep the symptoms from coming back.

Asthma attacks that are caused by allergens can be controlled with medications that treat allergy symptoms. Many people take antihistamines. Remember, histamine is the chemical that is released when the body is exposed to an allergen. It is the main cause of inflammation, runny nose, sneezing, itchy eyes, and other allergy symptoms. An antihistamine blocks the harmful effects of histamine. Some antihistamines don't start working until up to 30 minutes after you take them. And they may not be fully effective for one to two hours. If you take an antihistamine before you are exposed to the allergen, you can actually stop the allergic reaction before the symptoms appear. Antihistamines work well when they are taken regularly.

Another kind of allergy drug, cromolyn sodium, works by stopping the sensitive cells in the airways from reacting to allergens. They do not spill out histamine, and inflammation does not develop. However, this drug may take up to four weeks to become fully effective. It is better for preventing allergy symptoms rather than quick relief after they have started.

Some patients with allergies and moderate to severe asthma cannot control their condition with steroids.

A drug called Xolair® might be the answer. This allergy medicine works to block the antibodies that react with allergens, thus preventing an allergic reaction. A doctor needs to inject Xolair® into the patient once or twice a month. This is a long-term medicine, not for quick relief. Patients who take it usually have fewer asthma attacks and need less medication to control their asthma symptoms.

Decongestants are drugs that reduce swelling in the nasal passages. They help clear a stopped-up nose so that you can breathe more easily.

Handy Healthy Fact

Hot Stuff
Does eating chili or salsa make your nose run? If you have asthma, that may be a good thing. Scientists have found that hot peppers make the airways produce more fluid. This flushes out mucus and makes it easier to breathe.

AHHH!!

7

PREVENTING ASTHMA ATTACKS

The only sure way to be asthma-free, or at least reduce your risk of asthma attacks, is to avoid the triggers. For example, if you are allergic to a food, you should not eat it. If you are allergic to dust mites, remove all rugs and curtains from your bedroom and use dust-proof covers on your mattress and pillow. Staying away from cigarette smoke can also help you avoid bringing on an asthma attack.

This boy is using a hay fever helmet to avoid inhaling pollen and dust outside.

Secondhand Smoke

Studies have shown that smoking is not only bad for the smoker, it is also harmful to anybody who is around that person. Secondhand smoke—the smoke that people around a smoker breathe—can be very dangerous for someone with asthma. Smokers who have children with asthma should never smoke around their children. Even smoking in the same house can leave harmful chemicals that can linger for hours. Breathing secondhand smoke can trigger an asthma attack. The attack can be serious enough to send the child to the hospital.

If your allergies come at certain times of the year, try to stay indoors during those times. This is especially helpful in the middle of the day when pollen counts are usually the highest. Keep the windows closed so that the pollen and mold spores do not get into the house. Use air-conditioning instead. An air cleaner with a HEPA filter can help reduce allergens in your house all year round. This device takes allergens out of the air.

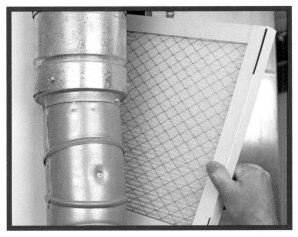
Filters can remove allergens from the air in homes and buildings.

One way to stop asthma attacks before they start is by taking asthma medication every day, as mentioned in the previous chapter. This is important if you need quick-relief medication more than two to three times a week.

People whose breathing problems are triggered by allergens can prevent asthma attacks by getting allergy shots. Each shot contains a tiny amount of an allergen. When it is injected, some of the allergen gets into the blood and causes the body to make special antibodies for that allergen. These new antibodies, called blocking antibodies, are different from the ones that produce allergic reactions. They "block" the allergic reaction by grabbing the allergen and keeping it from reacting with allergy antibodies.

Each injection contains a little more of the allergen, and more blocking antibodies are made. After a while, there is enough of the blocking antibody to tie up the allergen and keep it from causing trouble. Your body is now desensitized, and the allergen no longer triggers an allergic reaction.

Asthma does not have to control your life. Sometimes it may be tough trying to live your life without worrying about something bringing on an attack. But with the support of your doctor and family, you can gain control over your asthma. It may take some time, but you will learn to live a full life, with asthma just a part of it.

Allergy shots can help many people avoid reactions and attacks.

GLOSSARY

allergen—A substance that causes an allergic reaction. Plant pollens and foods are common examples.

allergy—An overreaction of the immune system to a normally harmless substance.

alveoli (sing. alveolus)—The tiny air sacs in the lungs, where gas exchange takes place.

antibodies—Special proteins produced by white blood cells. Some antibodies help kill germs.

antihistamine—A drug that stops the effects of histamine, which produces allergy symptoms.

asthma—A disease in which the air passages in the lungs become inflamed, making breathing difficult.

blocking antibodies—Antibodies that prevent allergic reactions by tying up allergens and keeping them from reacting with allergy antibodies.

bronchi (sing. bronchus)—The larger air tubes of the lungs.

bronchioles—The smaller air tubes of the lungs that branch off from the bronchi.

bronchodilator—A drug that opens the airways during an asthma attack.

bronchospasm—A sudden, brief narrowing of the muscles in the airway walls.

cilia—Tiny hairlike structures in the lining of the airways that move back and forth, sweeping foreign particles out and up to the throat.

cromolyn sodium—An allergy drug that works by stopping the sensitive cells in the airways from reacting to allergens.

dander—Flakes of dead skin from animals.

decongestant—A drug that reduces swelling in the breathing passages.

desensitize—To make a person's body stop overreacting to an allergen.

diagnose—To identify a condition from its signs and symptoms.

dust mites—Microscopic bugs that feed on the flakes of dead skin in house dust.

histamine—A chemical released in the body that causes tissues to become inflamed in an allergic reaction.

immune system—The body's disease-fighting system, including white blood cells.

inflammation—Redness and swelling as a result of damage or an allergic reaction.

lungs—Two baglike organs used for breathing.

mucus—A gooey liquid produced by cells in the lining of the nose and breathing passages.

nebulizer—A device that turns liquid into a spray; a type of inhaler.

peak flow meter—A handheld device that measures how fast air flows out of the lungs when a person exhales quickly.

RAST test—A blood test for specific kinds of antibodies to show sensitivity to particular allergens.

respiratory system—The organs involved in breathing, from the nose to the lungs.

sensitization—The development of an allergy after repeated exposure to an allergen.

spirometer—A machine that measures how much air goes in and out of a person's airways.

steroid—A type of anti-inflammatory drug.

trachea—The windpipe; a breathing tube that connects the nose and throat to the bronchi.

trigger—A substance or condition (such as dust or a cold) that brings on an asthma attack.

wheeze—A whistling sound heard when a person breathes through narrowed airways.

white blood cells—Jellylike blood cells that are an important part of the body's defenses. Some white blood cells eat germs and clean up bits of damaged cells and dirt.

LEARN MORE

Books

Landau, Elaine. *Asthma*. Tarrytown, N.Y.: Marshall Cavendish Benchmark, 2009.

Paquette, Penny Hutchins. *Asthma: The Ultimate Teen Guide*. Lanham, Md.: Scarecrow Press, 2006.

Royston, Angela. *Explaining Asthma*. Mankato, Minn.: Smart Apple Media, 2010.

Weiss, Jonathan H. *Breathe Easy: Young People's Guide to Asthma*. Washington, D.C.: Magination Press, 2003.

Web Sites

TeensHealth: Asthma Basics
    <http://kidshealth.org/teen/asthma_center/>

Just for Kids: Allergies and Asthma
    <http://www.aaaai.org/conditions-and-treatments/just-for-kids.aspx>

INDEX

A
air pollution, 6, 25, 31
allergen, 19, 21, 22, 23, 32, 33, 38, 39, 41, 42, 43
allergies, 17, 18, 19, 21, 25, 31, 33, 38, 41
allergy shot, 42
alveoli, 9
antibodies, 18, 19, 20, 21, 33, 39, 42, 43
asthma
  attack, 6, 7, 12, 15, 16, 17, 18, 22, 23, 25, 26, 32, 33, 34, 35, 37, 38, 39, 40, 41, 42, 43
  causes, 12, 13, 14, 17, 18, 19, 21, 23, 24, 38
  diagnosing, 29, 30, 31, 32, 33
  preventing attacks, 6, 15, 35, 38, 39, 40–43
  symptoms, 13–15, 20, 21–22, 29, 38
  treating, 6, 34–39
  trigger, 17, 22, 23, 25, 32, 33, 40

B
blood, 7, 18, 27, 33, 42
breathing, 5, 6, 7–11, 13–14, 16, 30, 41, 42
bronchi, 8, 9
bronchial tubes, 12, 13

C
chemicals, 19–20, 21, 23, 25, 27, 38, 41
cigarettes, 25, 27, 40
cilia, 11, 15, 27
cold, 6, 24, 25–26
cough, 6, 11, 14–15, 29

D
dander, 22
doctor, 12, 30–31, 34, 36, 37, 39, 43
dust, 6, 10, 11, 12, 18, 19, 22, 24, 33, 40
dust mites, 24, 40

E
emphysema, 27
exercise, 6, 8, 25, 28

F
food, 19–20, 23, 40

H
heart, 27, 30
histamine, 21–22, 38

I
immune system, 18, 19, 21
inhaler, 34–35

L
lungs, 7–8, 9, 10, 11, 12, 14, 15, 25, 27, 33

M
medication, 6, 32, 34–35, 37–39, 42
mold, 6, 22, 24, 41
mucus, 10–11, 13, 14, 26, 27, 39

N
nebulizer, 34

O
oxygen, 7, 10, 25, 27

P
peak flow meter, 33
pollen, 6, 11, 18, 19, 22, 24, 41

R
rash, 20
RAST test, 33
respiratory illnesses, 25, 29, 31
respiratory system, 8

S
sensitization, 20
skin, 21, 22, 24, 32
smoke, 12, 25, 27, 31, 41
sneezing, 11, 17, 22, 24, 38
spirometer, 30, 32
steroid, 37, 38

T
throat, 8, 15, 27
treating asthma, 6, 34–39

W
wheezing, 6, 12, 13, 14, 29
white blood cells, 18, 21